D1611811

HALFWAY
FROM
HOXIE

BOOKS BY MILLER WILLIAMS

POETRY

A Circle of Stone
Recital
So Long at the Fair
The Only World There Is
Halfway from Hoxie

TRANSLATIONS FROM THE POETRY
OF NICANOR PARRA

Poems and Antipoems
(with contributions from other translators)
Emergency Poems

ANTHOLOGIES

19 Poetas de Hoy en los EEUU
Southern Writing in the Sixties: Poetry
(with John William Corrington)
Southern Writing in the Sixties: Fiction
(with John William Corrington)
Chile: An Anthology of New Writing
Contemporary Poetry in America

CRITICAL STUDIES

The Achievement of John Ciardi
The Poetry of John Crowe Ransom

HALFWAY
FROM
HOXIE

new & selected poems

MILLER WILLIAMS

E. P. DUTTON & CO., INC.   NEW YORK 1973

Library of Congress Cataloging in Publication Data

Williams, Miller.
Halfway from Hoxie.

I. Title.   55339
PS3545.I53352H3   811'.5'4   73-78330
ISBN 0-525-12035-1
ISBN 0-525-03525-7 (pbk.)

Published simultaneously in Canada by Clarke, Irwin & Company
Limited, Toronto and Vancouver
SBN: 0–525–12035–1
Library of Congress Catalog Card Number: 73–78330

GRATEFUL ACKNOWLEDGMENT IS MADE TO THE PUBLICATIONS
IN WHICH THE FOLLOWING POEMS FIRST APPEARED:

THE AMERICAN SCHOLAR
The Associate Professor Delivers an Exhortation to His Failing Students
The Assoc. Professor (Mad Scientist) to (His Love) His Student in Physics
   100 Lab
Weatherman

ANTAEUS
Hurrah for the Fun Is the Pudding Done Hurrah for the Pumpkin Pie

ANTIOCH REVIEW
Sale

BLACK BOX
To Becky with Love the Eighth Year of the Slaughter
Problems in the Space-Time Continuum
And Then

BROWN PAPER BAG
A Letter to Cindy, Robert & Karen

CHICAGO REVIEW
The Woman on the Porch

CONCERNING POETRY
The House in the Vacant Lot

CRAZY HORSE
Cabbala

DECEMBER
Voice of America

DENVER QUARTERLY
The 20th Anniversary of the Ed Sullivan Show . . .
How a Sparrow Was Caught in My Trap . . .
Love Poem

THE DICKINSON REVIEW
Leaving New York on the Penn Central to Metuchen
Think of Judas that He Did Love Jesus
Vision and Prayer
For Kenneth Patchen
On the Symbolic Consideration of Hands . . .

EPOS
Euglena
For Clement Long, Dead, Lines Written in the Dark (originally titled "Lines
    Written in the Dark")

THE FALCON
Side Show
In Your Own Words Without Lying . . .
During A Language Lesson: For Karen

GENESIS WEST
On the Death of a Middle-Aged Man

JEOPARDY
Let Me Tell You
Vs the People
Thinking Friday Night with a Gothic Storm Going . . .

THE MEDITERRANEAN REVIEW
I Go Out of the House for the First Time

MOTIVE
A Note to God Concerning a Point from . . .
And When in Scenes of Glory

THE NEW YORK TIMES BOOK REVIEW MAGAZINE
Countdown

NIMROD
For Lucy, On Her Birthday

NORTHWEST REVIEW
Think Also of Horseshoes

THE OBERLIN QUARTERLY
Notes in a Minister's Hymnbook

PAN AMERICAN REVIEW
La Ultima Carta

POETRY NORTHWEST
Put Out the Phoenix
A Toast to Floyd Collins

PRAIRIE SCHOONER
Plain

PREVIEW
To Lucy, On the Brink

RAVEN
Vision in Black and White

SATURDAY REVIEW
On the Death of the Veteran
Done to His Mistress
The Widow
Log

SHENANDOAH
Accident: A Short Story

SOUTHERN HUMANITIES REVIEW
Guided Tour

SOUTHERN POETRY REVIEW
Of Human Bondage

THE TEXAS QUARTERLY
Home from a Party after Having Been Told Again . . . (Originally titled
    "On Reading How an Electronic Computer Can Win at Chess")
Depot in a River Town

THE VIRGINIA QUARTERLY
It Is Not that It Came to Nothing Emiliano

THE WEST COAST POETRY REVIEW
The Neighbor
If I Said I Love You Would You? No.

For Becky

CONTENTS

from *A CIRCLE OF STONE* (1964)

For Robert, *Son of Man*   3

Original Sin   4

Home from a Party after Having Been Told Again
How Perfectly Good the World Is Going to Be   5

On the Death of the Veteran   6

For Lucy, *On Her Birthday*   8

On the Death of a Middle-Aged Man   9

Depot in a River Town   11

The Woman on the Porch   12

Notes in a Minister's Hymnbook   15

The Associate Professor Delivers an Exhortation
to His Failing Students   17

from *SO LONG AT THE FAIR* (1968)

A Note to God Concerning a Point
from an Earlier Communication   23

Weatherman   25

Think Also of Horseshoes   27

The Caterpillar   28

And When in Scenes of Glory   30

Euglena   34

Taxi Drivers Know Everything   35

For Clement Long, *Dead, Lines Written in the Dark*   37

Countdown   38

Guided Tour   39

To Lucy, *On the Brink*   42

Done to his Mistress   43

The Writer   44

Put Out the Phoenix   47

Of Human Bondage   48

Accident: *A Short Story*   49

The Widow   52

Sale   54

The Man at the Blue Movie   56

Cat You Do Not   58

from *THE ONLY WORLD THERE IS* (1971)

Let Me Tell You   61

Today Is Wednesday   63

Side Show   65

La Ultima Carta: *A Young Venezuelan Wife Writes
to Her Husband in the Mountains*   69

It Is Not that It Came to Nothing Emiliano   72

Log   73

Plain   74

July 20, 1969   75

In Commemoration of the 20th Anniversary
of the Ed Sullivan Show
and Every Anniversary Following   83

How a Sparrow Was Caught in My Trap
when I Was Ten
and Covered with Lice so I Killed It   86

Voice of America   87

Vs the People   89

How the Elephant Got His Hump   92

The House in the Vacant Lot   97

If Every Person There Is But One   99

The Assoc. Professor (Mad Scientist)
to (His Love) His Student
in Physics 100 Lab   101

I Have Never   103

In Your Own Words Without Lying
Tell Something of Your Background
with Particular Attention
to Anything Relating to the Position
for Which You Are Now Applying: Press Down   105

My Father Who Is Seventy-Five
Will Not Thank God for His Years   109

During a Language Lesson: For Karen   110

At the End of My Thirty-ninth Year   111

A Letter to Cindy, Robert & Karen   113

Love Poem   116

NEW POEMS

Leaving New York on the Penn Central to Metuchen   121

Think of Judas that He Did Love Jesus   123

Thinking Friday Night with a Gothic Storm Going
about Final Causes and Logos and Mitzi Mayfair   126

If I Said I Love You Would You? No.   129

To Becky with Love
the Eighth Year of the Slaughter   130

Hurrah for the Fun
Is the Pudding Done
Hurrah for the Pumpkin Pie   131

Vision and Prayer   133

Remembering Walter   134

For Kenneth Patchen   135

Problems in the Space-Time Continuum:
Undiscovered Letter to Mitzi Mayfair   136

And Then   137

The Neighbor   138

Cabbala   139

I Go Out of the House for the First Time   141

A Toast to Floyd Collins   142

On the Symbolic Consideration of Hands
and the Significance of Death   143

Vision in Black and White   144

from *A Circle of Stone*

FOR ROBERT, *Son of Man*

With eyes that have found the rain and first stars
you looked from your face to my face
Robert . . . son
What are these for?
your manhood held in your fingers
where frogs and rocks were held
in the wild yards.

Then your great things were boulders coming down
tumbling from some cold and holy place
What are these for?
loudly through centuries
to find me here in this Buck Rogers town

this year in this Roy Rogers room, with you,
holding your name, looking at my long look
What are these for?
I'm full of lies to tell
to a boy of five half-Christian and half-Jew.

Rolling from where it tumbled when you spoke
the answer comes ochre and smelling of earth
and we are together
in a circle of stone
where the sun slips red and new
to a stand of oak.

ORIGINAL SIN

Wednesday nights
I walked in shadows past prayer meeting lights
and gave my time
for an hour and a half at the movies
and god's dime.

I was scared
when the girl who sold the tickets because she was dared
by a man as old
as my father let me feel.
She was cold

and this surprise
was my revelation—but I made lies
and looking at her
twisted my mouth as if it
didn't matter.

In bed my hand
was cold still and the fingers I let pretend
that she was lying
white on a blue hill,
birds flying.

Slowly wrong
I love my wife a time and the night long
I feel the hair
of a high girl grinning red
a night of prayer.

HOME FROM A PARTY
AFTER HAVING BEEN TOLD AGAIN
HOW PERFECTLY GOOD THE WORLD
IS GOING TO BE

There is something wandering in my town
out of the shadows with an old man's face.

At home are the lonely walkers.
The birds hold a tightening silence
and dogs scratch on all doors to be let in.

The bolder men take slowly to the streets
keep to the other side
and move a block before him
wonderfully backwards.

Loudspeaker blaring from the slow soundtruck
the mayor says the monkey is a friend

but I can't stop running
and looking back I see him dancing toward me

gifts in his hands.

ON THE DEATH OF THE VETERAN

It wasn't history
Vicksburg and Manassas when I went to bed
because he was with us here in the same block
no more than my brother's birthday
because you can touch it
because remembering is one thing
and history is another

I never thought of it as the past
the way I never think of Greenland as distant
because I know a soldier who was there

but I read the *Telegraph* at breakfast
and saw that no one's been there anymore

and I thought someone ought to pray for a man
before another argument comes up
when Lees go down in the fall of their great horses
and Grants four starred and beardless
rise as serious as Christ
and drop like spit

to read the passing of the last of us
and say putting his coffee on the table
well it's history
as if he'd found molasses gone to sugar
and love us for it

to pray for his son
that his son forget our battles
recalling to the classrooms and those green windows
only the everlasting Saturdays

that terror be something told of
a word from the old ways
or down his father's own dark street
faces out of a movie and bad dreams

FOR LUCY, *On Her Birthday*

Were you born as I was, beautiful witch?

I think you were spun by spiders
on a black mountain.

How woman were you I took as only woman
then there was magic, and before I knew
you were wind and dust and summer days
rain across the window
cold and holy water

and white fire.

What can I bring, extraordinary woman?
Wings of bats

or moon dark?

ON THE DEATH OF A MIDDLE-AGED MAN

Beverly
who wished his mother wanting a girl again
had called him something at best ambiguous
like Francis or Marion
went for fifteen years to the Packard plant
and turned for Helen who punched proper holes
the bumperless bodies.

He took her
to dinner once and left her notes in secret
when hair fell down to his forehead and refused
the foreman's job.

Except for
when she was seven her brother which couldn't count
when she was twelve the preacher and that was for God
she never did nothing

Christ would have died for.
Going home
before the coffin was lowered because of the clouds
he fell in front of a car because of the rain.
There were just enough
to bear him
counting the foreman a man from the shift a cousin
come to lay claim.

A woman played the piano.
A minister who kept forgetting his name
said he was forgiven
that he would be forever
at the bosom of Abraham
which was the preacher's way of saying heaven.

DEPOT IN A RIVER TOWN

In the depot and the darkened day
the clack of an old pinball machine
demands a curious notice.
More sleeping than not
a satchel faced farmer makes noises.
A sailor circles like a child in church.

In the depot and the darkened day
I surrender my back to the imperative bench,
unlistening hear the emphatic pencil
tap itself on the table.

The little blonde reads
and fingers the cloth of her blouse
like a nun telling beads.

Cracked across after an ancient painting
the face of the woman with children
ignores and ignores.
There is fog at the windows
and the open doors.

Within the ear's rim rises a separate sound.
Wood slapping side slipping water sounds
settle me deep.
I feel again the penny in my pocket
and the slow sleep of the river
wraps me round.

11

THE WOMAN ON THE PORCH

You would have said
if you could have seen her there
skin of a cow's udder hung beneath her eyes

you would have said
your loveliness is lost

left in paper bags beside your husband
black with pigs' blood and the waters of your children

you move your lips as if they have lost one another
touching and touching
like blind ants coming together

you make the sound breathing
you would say
of rats running.

If you had gone back to the gate
holding her there in your eyes
and that house

the chair she rocked in and the shoes coming clump
to the floor

if you could have known
if it had come to you
what she was doing

that she was all the rocking around the earth
that she drove rocking all the back and forth
up down and open shut all came from here
that she was every breathing and fish gill
rope skip run go in and out the window

spring and ratchet for every come and go
swing me high let the cat die
prayer wheeling prince
do it fast and fistly
rock-tock for all the trot a horse
and woah

hardtit twelve and lover housewife and whore
go together backseat bed and floor.

From here funeral home fans
moved the air in buzzing Sunday heat
swept flies from faces closed on sleep
and kept communion
between the sermon and the falling thoughts.

If knowing as I did she knew
she had looked at you
changing her face to knowledge I could not stand
would you not have killed her

if you had seen her on the deceiving porch
of ordinary wood crawled through by weeds

rocking only as fast as I could breathe?

(there are spiders who spin your name
if you tell a lie
and when they finish the letters
you have to die)

Because there is truth not to be believed
or if known denied
I did it
before the nibbling lips had split
to the turned-in toothless grin of recognition

(the sea sinks after ships that drown
to make a mouth the boats are swallowed down)

And a hand more thin than a bird's wing motioned me in
offered the empty bladder of her bust
and a place where knowledge was and forgotten vision
pulled at me like whirlpools and god's lust.

NOTES IN A MINISTER'S HYMNBOOK

This science thing
that ought to have destroyed poetry
tells us our lives may yet be in the stars
that would with laws and logic kill the witch
finds cause for healing in a faithful hand
fertility in the moon
my table a spirit.

How can I tell if half the saints were mad
or Paul (Saul) conned us?
I itch I know and scratch my flesh in pleasure
go wild upon my wife and imagine yours

suspect that I may go the way I came
into waters I will have forgotten
and not a drop of water know my name.

I conjure all the hells that I could go to
and the Hindu nil becomes considerable.
I have read of redemption—
when Jonah washed at the shore of the cryptic sea
from his flesh the smell of the vomit of fish
and the feel
when the whore seven times undressed
in the bright door
and found her thighs naked by day were clean
when Lot stopped hearing his woman's
hard breathing behind him
and hurried on—

so heaven I know is harder than confession
or hope or love or luck or the ritual act;
the bright waters of Pilate are unpoured
here in this confounded and holy room
and the pains of Judas are useless and not mine.

Christ made miracles by Galilee
and God sent ghosts and simple peasants
saw them.
I have only seen ladies riding horses
and once in Arkansas
a brown boy eating froglegs
cooked in a hubcap.

None of his names was Jesus.

THE ASSOCIATE PROFESSOR
DELIVERS AN EXHORTATION
TO HIS FAILING STUDENTS

Now when the frogs
that gave their lives for nothing
are washed from the brains and pans
we laid them in
I leave to you
who most excusably misunderstand
the margins of my talks
which because I am wise
and am a coward
were not appended to the syllabus

but I will fail to tell you
what I tell you
even before you fail to understand
so we might
in a manner of speaking
go down together.

I should have told you something of importance
to give at least a meaning
to the letter:

how, after hope, it sometimes happens

a girl, anonymous as beer,
telling forgotten things in a cheap bar

how she could have taught here as well as I.
Better.

The day I talked about the conduction of currents
I meant to say
be careful about getting hung up in the brain's things
that send you screaming like madmen through the town
or make you
like the man in front of the Jungle
that preaches on Saturday afternoons
a clown.

The day I lectured on adrenalin
I meant to tell you
as you were coming down
slowly out of the hills of certainty

empty your mind of the hopes that held you there.
Make a catechism of all your fears

and say it over:

this is the most of you . . . who knows . . . the best
where God was born
and heaven and confession
and half of love

From the fear of falling
and being flushed away
to the gulp of the suckhole and that rusting gut
from which no Jonah comes

that there is no Jesus and no hell

that God
square root of something equal to all
will not feel the imbalance when you fall

that rotting you will lie unbelievably alone
to be sucked up by some insignificant oak
as a child draws milk through straws
to be his bone.

These are the gravity that holds us together
toward our common sun

every hope getting out of hand
slings us hopelessly outward one by one
till all that kept us common is undone.

The day you took the test
I would have told you this:
that you had no time to listen for questions
hunting out the answers in your files
is surely the kind of irony
poems are made of

that all the answers at best are less than half

and you would have remembered
Lazarus
who hung around with God or the devil for days
and nobody asked him

anything

But if they do
If one Sunday morning they should ask you

the only thing that matters after all
tell them the only thing you know is true

tell them failing is an act of love
because
like sin
it is the commonality within

how failing together we shall finally pass
how to pomp and circumstance all of a class
noble of eye, blind mares between our knees,
lances ready, we ride to Hercules.

The day I said this had I meant to hope
some impossible punk on a cold slope
stupidly alone
would build himself a fire
to make of me an idiot

and a liar

from *So Long at the Fair*

A NOTE TO GOD CONCERNING A POINT
FROM AN EARLIER COMMUNICATION

Baseball players know the meaning of sacrifice
so did St. Francis
Jesus on the cross
Judas hanged
so do monks keeping their mouths shut forever
nuns sleeping alone.

The choice was easy and the burden light
because the other way was harder than possible.
Nuns are faithful to a husband who is rich
and the monks have partnership
in a damned good deal.

That Sir is the point.
We invest ourselves always in some Return.
Sacrifice is a way of winning
and we have misnamed it.

But Sir I wonder
if there is no way I can deny myself
and everything we give we give in trade
what is sin but witless bargaining
and virtue but a good eye for horses
and a taste for mansions.

I am aware things are done in mysterious ways
and only ask.

You will call it doubt
but Sir you would not believe

how very much it seems like the old praise
you would recall from Pentecostal days

a confusion of tongues.

WEATHERMAN

He was always there
a clumsy grammared hick with a crooked tie
and we turned him on
the way we scrub before meals
and say grace
when no one clearly needs it but in case
of unlikely plagues
the visitation of demons or an evil eye.

We tolerated his talk of a sky not ours
followed his endless scribbling on the wall
because it's best to be if possible
unsurprised by rain.

The hurricane came
was coming
and only that face
transported out of space to the living glass
could tell us how close it was
when it turned like a mad ghost to the north
and smelled our streets.

On that late September afternoon
when the sky was sagging heavy with sandbags
before the box he was blocked in like a household shrine
we offered him our faith
pledged to buy Pepsi
commended our homes and children
into his hand,

25

followed the scrawl
he wiggled and tapped across the bright wall
knew there was sense we didn't understand
were almost sure
by making the marks over the shape of our state
he could conjure the wind back to the water
the water from the land.

We listened believing
and when it fell around us
we rode it out on his words
two and three tight in a dark room
his transistored voice disembodied
the miraculous pictures in the miraculous past.

And when it was gone
after we dragged the fallen tree away
and cleaned the walk
and put the window in
we were a town
of forty thousand people
who had been a worship
and a fear.
He was a man
who kept a ritual
we suffered him
after the news.

THINK ALSO OF HORSESHOES

Look at the nails on the wall
study the straight line
think of the man who hammered them years ago
he was a delta buck with a fat wife

Look at the tailgate bang on the back of a truck
think about the man who put it there
think of his daughter failing the fifth grade

Unwrap a cigar
think of the man who planted the tobacco
think of his dog peeing on the plants

Turn a rusty bottle cap out of the ground
think of the boy who drank the strawberry soda
think of him delivering *The Democrat*
chased by the dog run over
today by the truck
made by the man lost in Michigan
whose daughter is misspelling words for a Jew teacher
who writes *True Confessions* for the fat wife
of the diligent carpenter who is dead now.

THE CATERPILLAR

Today on the lip of a bowl in the backyard
we watched a caterpillar caught in the circle
of his larval assumptions

my daughter counted
27 times he went around
before rolling back and laughing
I'm a caterpillar, look
she left him
measuring out his slow green way to some place
there must have been a picture of inside him

After supper
coming from putting the car up
we stopped to look
figured he crossed the yard
once every hour
and left him
when we went to bed
wrinkling no closer to my landlord's leaves
than when he somehow fell to his private circle

Later I followed
barefeet and doorclicks of my daughter
to the yard   the bowl
a milkwhite moonlight eye
in the black grass

it died

I said honey they don't live very long

In bed again
re-covered and re-kissed
she locked her arms and mumbling love to mine
until turning she slipped
into the deep bone-bottomed dish
of sleep

Stumbling drunk around the rim
I hold
the words she said to me across the dark

I think he thought he was
going in a straight line

AND WHEN IN SCENES OF GLORY

When I had been born eight years I was born again
washed in the waters of life
and saved from hell
from the devil the Baptists the Campbellites
and the Pope

When I was told about Santa Claus and the sun
and learned for myself
that trees feel their leaves fall off
and scream at night

I thought about Jesus Christ who had long hair
was hung by the hands
buried and came alive

(in the Roxy Saturday afternoons
rag-dragging zombies came alive in caves
the blood of people made them live forever)

God come down

With hands that could have torn the hills apart
the preacher hammered the tinfoil of my faith
and words came teaching me
out of the terrible whirlwind of his mouth
the taste of evil
bitter and hot as belch
the agony of God

building the gospel word by believable word
out of the wooden syllables of the South

God come down

and over the pews over the dry domes
amens rose up like birds
beating the air for heaven
heading for home and roost
in the right eye

come for the sake of Jesus

and the white thigh
of Mrs. Someone sitting in the choir

Over the altar
over the lilies the grapejuice and the bread
was The Resurrection

boy do you believe

I looked to see if the Romans had
marks on their necks

in Jesus Christ his only son our Lord

Yes Sir I do
A woman so skinny I could smell her bones
hugged me because I'd turned away from sin

Going home at night after the preaching
after prayers and dinner on the ground
curling in the backseat of the car

I began to feel like a thickening of the dark
almost my mother talking to my father
almost my father singing to himself
my name a gospel song
and a long applause like gravel under the tires

until I heard the wings
and knew it had come
what I had killed and couldn't come anymore
to hunger against the black glass of the car
the thing you think what would happen
if you saw its face

I'd have prayed to God not to have a flat
but God would have laughed
and it would have sounded like
the flapping of wings
over the old Dodge
over the grinding of gravel
and the hymn of grace

Floating with fishes under the river of sound
I remembered with my last dull thought
before I drowned
that I was saved from sin and the world was lost

The river stopped
and the world stopped
and I am lifted up

to be dropped again by my father
onto an unmade bed in a borrowed room
to play the old parable
like the flipping pictures in the penny arcade

falling over and over dime by dime
to wait my ankles crossed holding my breath
a dumb kid in some silly game
for the law straining around the earth to crack
and the rock roll back

Monday morning we had oatmeal for breakfast
After school Ward West kicked the piss out of me
Tuesday it snowed

EUGLENA

Microscopic monster
germ father, founder of the middle way
who first saw fit to join no clan
but claim the best of both
you are more than clever.

Swimming, you go to what meal is.
Green, you make what isn't.

Fencerider
mimicked by more than have heard of
Jesus or Nietzsche

you've held your own for twenty
million years

who might have been a tulip
or a tiger

you shrewd little bastard

TAXI DRIVERS KNOW EVERYTHING

Taxi drivers know everything

The address of a whorehouse
               a museum
               an abortionist

Where you can buy beer on Sunday
               berets
               bennies
               dildoes even

The best restaurants

The headquarters of the American
               Academy of Poets
               the Black Muslims
               the Minutemen

Where you can find a little action
               a fence
               a brain surgeon
               a priest
               a pusher
               a masochist

In New York
taxi drivers know everything
except what I ask them:

What if you were Jonah and your taxi
was a whale?
What if I was your mother and I
caught you?
What if Judas had been faithful?
What if you woke up?

I always leave a quarter on the seat.

FOR CLEMENT LONG, *Dead,*
Lines Written in the Dark

Lord listen, or heaven is undone.
He will not spell your name or take your hand,
will hee-haw at the gate with a held breath,
will run away to the end where death is real.

Lord if you chase him like a wheatfield fire
till hallelujahs and a choir of angels
sing him coming and the grand gates open,
still he will stand against your house
where no sin ever is and no flesh fails.

If even he has treasures, let the mouse
discover the grain, take the worm to the tree.
Give his potential pleasures to the poor.
Or watch him. And watch him well. And watching see
how he subverts the angels, whispering this:

ninety and nine returned and deserve attending;
surely the faithful one, the unoffending
son should have the calf; God, it's a small grace
to be a counter of coins in the first place.

COUNTDOWN

Synchronize the falling clocks
Wind the mind and check the locks
Pick-up sticks and building blocks

pyramid to perfect knowing
minus ten and time is growing
small at nine is cold and snowing

eight is wheels and seven rain
what equation can explain
going backward in the brain

GUIDED TOUR

Ladies and gentlemen
please be seated
We are about to start.
Pay attention and nobody gets hurt.

The Statue of Liberty is the
first point of interest.
Note the inscription: We Fix Things.

On the left
three blind preachers
playing guitars and chanting
Farther Along.

There you see a girl
fixing her face.

This is a garbage can.

On the left you see a green woman
with one leg
sitting on a nailkeg
knitting a butterfly.

On the right is the flag.
Also on the left is the flag.

In the National Bank
you can see the assistant cashier
fixing the books.

Please do not look out the window
with your eyes closed
as the windows are rented only
for this trip.

On the right is the Church of Jesus
farther along we'll know more about it
farther along we'll understand why

I direct your attention back of the blue door
You see two lovers moving on the couch
He is smothering her with a pillow
The only words in the room are on the pillow:
Sister
Camp Chaffee
1943

On the right is a man in a Mustang
He is fixing a ticket
without getting out of his car
This is made possible by progress
and your tax-paying investor-owned mayor.

On the left is the True Church of Jesus
cheer up my brother live in the sunshine
we'll understand it all by and by

Notice the boy
writing eschatological lyrics
on the crapper wall.
He is writing in Aramaic.

On the right you see the Friends of People
clapping hands and dancing in a circle:
a dean of women
an undertaker
a christian businessman
a county sheriff
a social worker
a psychoanalyst
the president of a finance company
                of the Kiwanis Club
                of Sigma Chi
and Captain Kangaroo.
Can you see what they are doing now?
They are changing clothes with one another.

Far to the right the
Electric Corporation.
Observe the vice-president
fixing the prices.

Behind the furnace the janitor gives
a sine qua non to his woman.

There walking backward down the sidewalk
is my dead grandpa.

And straight ahead we have
two children
sitting in the street

His name is Dealer's Choice
Her name is also Dealer's Choice
They hold a snake in their hands
They have soft fingers
You must look quckly. We will soon
run over them.

41

TO LUCY, *On the Brink*

Can you hardly be so frightened
how so soft a grip has tightened
on my hand

are your fears so quickly deep
how you talk us out of sleep
how you stand

close to me as clothes allow you
closer then and more and how you
tumbling hold

How does nothing more than death
only running out of breath
wake you cold

Give them all the toy terrors
fire and fear and final errors
Here today

be my wine and I your bread
I your quilt and you my bed
and let them play

DONE TO HIS MISTRESS

If blood still flows and wanting it to stays with us
when losing touch
we take unthinkable forms,
if recalling this night is something to count on
there have not been any signs
my love.

How will we know when in the Christmas Corps
wearing our Xs like division patches
we see the cipher done
and are solved for

How will we know
when we are cubed and taken to our roots
alphas in some obscure calculus

how we have raised ourselves to infinite powers
what it meant for a while to have no meaning
what it was to be ourselves, surd.

Before we see
another apple in the significant tree
let us be busy
constant to our time and smaller lies
let us be true and perfectly
prove nothing.

THE WRITER

Straight, thin as a pencil
blue tied and double breasted
he looks at the buttons
on the librarian's blouse
reads the sign for silence
and waits for his books.

Saturday evening
Sunday afternoon
he comes by city bus
from the room he rents
Gentleman, settled
Bath and private entrance
No pets

inside an apple-crate
packed away
forgotten stacks of
stories, articles
A Spreading of Nets: A novel
How to Double Your Pay
The Sharpes of Sharpe County in the Great Depression

Now he takes his books to his regular chair
takes out his glasses
out of a child's satchel a handful of papers
stops to stare when the
pale librarian passes

puts them before him in a
perfect square.

He begins to write
reading as he goes:
Esperanto, Language Without a Country
Devised by Ludwig Zamenhof, a doctor

Shakes his head and scratches out the line
Looks at the long librarian when she appears
Sits and picks at his nose and reads the sign.

Saturday afternoon he travels by bus
to the grave his wife
has waited in for years.

Pleased and disappointed that he has come
he reads for her
careful that he is alone
another poem done to honor her name.

"I thought I might send that one to the *Atlantic*.
I have a better one but it isn't finished.
A lot of people read my poems now."

He stops at the gate
takes a pad from his pocket
across it in a clean italic hand
The History of Tombstones. Good idea.

Picks up the mail
Reads the return address
with a tired surprise

Makes a cup of coffee.
Calls his priest on the telephone and confesses.
Calls his wife on the telephone and cries.
Tonight he will go to all the toilets he can walk to,
The Trailways Depot and the Billups Station.
He will put a poem on every wall.

One day he will wait
to see who takes the poems
skin slick with waiting to know
as still as stone
one day he will lie under cover
until he comes
He will take him by the arm
and say

what will he say

Excuse me, Sir
John Sharpe was killed on a harrow in '37
My name is Dr. Ludwig Zamenhof
I have a better one but it isn't finished
My wife is rotting in heaven
I wrote it for her

PUT OUT THE PHOENIX

She had big ankles
hair on her palms and
bad teeth
and she said
am I not beautiful
I said yes
you are beautiful
but I love you

I am full of flies she said
I know I said but I do not love you

Oh Goody she said
then there is nothing to stop us

Nothing makes sense I said
Oh Goody she said
then there is nothing to stop us

You are a dream I said
Oh Goody she said
then there is nothing to stop us

OF HUMAN BONDAGE

In a phone booth
on 42nd Street
by secret to the death
transmogrifications
he came to be
whatever was called for

as many a night
between the click of Zippos
and the slow smoke
How do you do and
Very well thank you and you
you son of a bitch

he has brought pale women dying for love
to life
pumping into their hulls
his grand reluctance

and murdered their men

Not even Lois Lane knows for sure

ACCIDENT: *A Short Story*

I

Listening to Billy Graham
reading my way to a snake farm
live grizzly bear   two-headed cow
100 yards ahead
I saw the car
its private parts turned public
the wheels still spinning
reeling in the runners from all directions.
I found you mumbling blood to the bobwire fence
all of its blackbirds flown
hubcap at your head like a helmet
your leg full of ankles.

Between your coontail Buick
and your split woman
telling heaven her minor miseries
I did what I could: kneeled as if I knew
what the balloons around us thought I knew

to call an ambulance: someone ran around
to drop a handkerchief
go in and out the window
find a phone.

II

I looked at my watch because it was late
because it was late I cursed you to hell

she is waiting and round
she is waiting and young
but here we are hung
your head in my hands
pieta in the dell.

Doctor. Preacher. Biblesalesman.
Man. There was nothing I could be.

How do you feel
Afraid
How do you feel
Cold
If I could have kept you alive
or blessed you
I would have stayed
but I was nothing to your old woman or you.
She knew it of course and kept calling for Jesus.
It was almost one
she would be gone by two
and so I left you
no worse off than you were

your puckered sockets sucking
the balls of your eyes
your lopsided head to a hand
it could fall to home in.
I looked for the heart behind me
pumping its light
into the hardened arteries of the air
the only thing there
was cudzu come to take the road again

III

At first you were something that happened
out of Natchez
and then you were something that happens every day
Damn you friend
and your wife
and your Buick car
(the time is one minute till five on all clocks).
Memory. Magician. Ghost. Whatever you are
I never saved your life
do not deserve
or want such faithfulness.

I did what I could

For weeks I turned through papers death by death
by Johnson by Givens by Washington Smith
at home
after an extended illness

survived by me

who is to blame
if the casual ambulance found
neither one of us waited

IV

Man. Unholy meat. Unfastened bones.
It was fifteen years ago and I stare still
at every blue suit with a broken face
wearing a hubcap, pulling a bad leg

I will start tomorrow reading the stones.

THE WIDOW

The Hammond Organ lubricates the air.
The kind mortician conducts her to her place
of honor. A man with a painted puppet's face
they say is her husband's face is obviously there

in front of her. She would have the casket
closed, but his sister would not. The minister cries
how gloriously the man is dead who lies
before him daily with a face like plastic,

prays that God who took him out of order
will keep his soul from torment, will adorn him
with a crown of stars, will hold with those that mourn him.
It is not hard, she thinks, but it will be harder.

The wail of the Hammond weakens, her mind goes black,
turning quickly out of the moment meanders
on curious ways. She looks at his nose. She wonders
if they went and slit the good blue suit in the back

and if his shoes are tied, if he has on
the socks they didn't ask for but she sent,
if they still use pennies, decides of course they don't,
hopes they will have their fill and be done with him soon.

It would not be fair to say she is not grieving.
She did not want to come, but she is aware
how there will be silence, there will be pleasures to bear
in silence, and dark creatures unbehaving.

She did not want to come. She will not be taken
to tears. But she is aware some moment will crush
the brain suddenly, that she will go home and wish
burglars had come there and the blind windows were broken.

SALE

Partnership dissolved.
Everything must be sold.
Individually or the set
as follows:

Brain, one standard, cold.
Geared to glossing.
Given to hard replies.
Convolutions convey the illusion
of exceptional depth.
Damaged.

think. think of me. but you are not thinking

One pair of eyes. Green. Like new.
Especially good for girls and women walking,
wicker baskets,
paintings by Van Gogh,
red clocks and frogs, chicken snakes and snow.

look at me. but you are not looking at me

One pair of ears, big. Best offer takes.
Tuned to Bach, Hank Williams, bees,
the Book of Job.
Shut-off for deans, lieutenants and
salesman talking.

listen. listen please. but you are not listening

Mouth, one wide.
Some teeth missing.
Two and a half languages. Adaptable to pipes
and occasional kissing.
Has been broken but in good repair.
Lies.

tell me. tell me please. why won't you tell me

Hands, right and left.
Feet. Neck. Some hair.
Stomach, heart, spleen and
accessory parts.

come. come quickly. there is only a little time

Starts tomorrow
what you've been waiting for
and when it's gone it's gone
so hurry

hurry

THE MAN AT THE BLUE MOVIE

A rattling machine
jerks the silent actors across the screen.

The creak of the floor
makes him remember he is not alone.
His brothers are here
names known and forgotten
from all the Friday nights he has come at nine
to sit for five bucks in a folding chair
above the Baptist mission on third street
for ten thin reels of unwinding passion
two hundred minutes
Mexican, German, Italian
American of course and even Russian
which doesn't make any difference
as nobody speaks.

He smiles at first
how much they are like home movies
This is Myrtle getting ready for bed
Look at Pearl and Pauline in the leather suits
Joe's daughter Melissa there with the high boots
and no maidenhead.

He looks from out of the night at the small square day
watches the clothes fall away
like forgiven sins
sees the chosen smiling blessed and kneeling
baptized and kissed.

Look how bright her face is
how blind the unsophisticated fingers

Around the room they start
to move like lizards
unaccountably
it breaks his heart

how round her body is
And full
How do you let him
He does not love you
at all

The last day flaps and rattles to a close.
The lights click on.
He chews the hard black nipple of his Bic.
His brothers suck on pipes and cigarettes.

The bored projectionist puts the machine away.
His wife takes down the screen
unlocks the door.

Quickly outside they scatter to pinball games
to children and wives. Ignore

the girls on the corner in the purple blouses.
He crosses the street
walks past the white fenced houses

to the city park
beyond the lighted tables where the old men play
believing that what he payed for was the dark.

CAT
YOU DO NOT

Cat
You do not drive cars
Cat
You do not read the newspaper
Cat
You sleep
You eat and drink milk
You catch cockroaches
and you sleep
Cat
You do not mail letters
Cat
You do not go to funerals
You sleep
across my lap
lying with everything shut
Cat
I am learning to sleep

from *The Only World There Is*

LET ME TELL YOU

how to do it from the beginning.
First notice everything:
The stain on the wallpaper
of the vacant house,
the mothball smell of a
Greyhound toilet.
Miss nothing. Memorize it.
You cannot twist the fact you do not know.

Remember
The blonde girl you saw in the spade bar.
Put a scar on her breast.
Say she left home to get away from her father.
Invent whatever will support your line.
Leave out the rest.

Use metaphors: The mayor is a pig
is a metaphor
which is not to suggest
it is not a fact.
Which is irrelevant.
Nothing is less important
than a fact.

Be suspicious of any word you learned
and were proud of learning.
It will go bad.
It will fall off the page.

When your father lies
in the last light
and your mother cries for him,
listen to the sound of her crying.
When your father dies
take notes
somewhere inside.

If there is a heaven
he will forgive you
if the line you found was a good line.

It does not have to be worth the dying.

TODAY IS WEDNESDAY

which is the day I have decided to understand.
I have tried since morning.
Now for the second time
my shadow is longer than I am
and still I can't understand.

I have asked everyone to help me.
I asked the busdriver to help me.
He said my name is John Foster Kelley
which is a name you will need.

I asked the waitress with mustard
on her mouth.
She said I have a surgical
scar on my belly.

I asked a policeman. I said
today is Wednesday.
He said go ask your mother.
I asked my mother.

I never saw you before in my life

son.

Tomorrow is Thursday.
Thursday I will understand.
If I can find the right bus
the right cafe

I will say
somebody help me.

Friday I will find myself
the one who can help me.

I will recognize it at once,
breasts of a big woman
face of a dog
the hinder parts held high
as a camel rises
in the unheated intergalactic spaces
under the gray blanket of my
most dry dreams

I will say *what about the whales*

and it will be done
Friday I will do it myself.

And I will tell everyone my understanding.
At first of course they will not hear
and when they do they will not allow me near
inhabited places.
I will grow old sending in scribbled notes
tied to the teats of cows and the tails of goats.

SIDE SHOW

Billboards sell me dirty miracles
the work of God gone bad.
Six girls their navels set with diadems
bumping their bottoms behind him
straddling invisible men not Methodists
the strawhatted preacher preaches
catches us running our tongues
around the girls.

eewolnks
eetolnks
eezalmos
chewmann
alive and breathing before your very
Look
(you think you got a skin problem
Lady
wait till you see the alligator woman)
fifty cents half a paper dollar.

The Alligator Woman
squats in her puddle
a dirty diaper slung
around her rear
an empty brassiere
pretending at the top
her legs crammed like crutches
into the hairy crotches of her arms.

She pulls at scabs
covering the best of her skin.
Something like milk leaks out.
She licks it away.

Hey over here
JoJo the Dogfaced Boy
found in the flats of Australia
naked and wild
by the famous Hiram Hinkleschitz
late of Harvard
raised by a band of marsupials
who took his mother
if you will forgive the expression
when she was a child.

JoJo barks
snaps at the legs
of a man and his giggling daughter
snarls how he could hurt
picks up his leg
against a post
makes the sound between his teeth
of dirt receiving water.

Fanny the Fat Lady
Fellows
Five hundred pounds a quarter
of a ton
the little bikini is bed sheets
put your misconceptions aside a second
try to imagine
you probably wonder how she got this way.

She was lithesome once as smoke
rising out of your house on a calm day.
She loved a man too much and when
she lost him
she consoled herself by feeding her flesh.
Her weight is a measure of her love.

The Fat Lady moves her face to a laugh and squeaks,
her glistening dugs move barely and slip back,
settle slowly, sleep soft and heavy
as slugs.
She crams a candy bar between her cheeks.

See the Siamese Twins the Inseparable Sisters:
See the one that has the frowning face.
Today is Thursday. Thursday is the day
for her to stumble backwards
to see the world jerk away.
Both of the ladies are virgins
I need not say
and they will be virgins
sleeping on their sides
the happy one careful
the sad one careful to scratch
no itch not her own by definition.

I don't like to mention
which is why I whisper
the next
well
person
out of respect for
consider

67

what must be the
lord
embarrassment
please do not stare
out of common respect
who has to earn a living
revealing those parts
I cannot mention for lord the innocent ears.

Something inside you've never dreamed of.

Friday morning
walking to work
I listen to each tap tell me
though girls are dancing everywhere I go
though the clouds hang loose from pole to pole
I walk on two legs in a world of sidewalks
and am real
and have a pedestrian and unprofitable soul.

LA ULTIMA CARTA: *A Young Venezuelan Wife*
Writes to Her Husband in the Mountains

I make a Y
brittle as dry wood.
The sputtering pen splits open
unwrites words I could not have mailed.

Saturday I sat by the lake
pretended to read letters
that have not come.
They are too brief and tell me you are well.
I am not sure I believe them.

Under my hand, Husband
brooms break
corn grinds to sand.

You have no faith in spirits
would claim the water
dripping from a tap at night
means nothing
that a wind coming down to the coast
out of those hills is neither alive nor dead
but I listen for signs

and forgive me this:
when the wind
brushes against the curtain
touches my sheet
I tense to feel the fingers of a ghost.

I look through my eyes in the morning mirror
afraid I will conjure you
trying to conjure you there
but all I see are the days spinning back
with the strange quiet violence of dreams.

Sra. Cortinez whose son was a good soldier
is also alone and knows she is going
to be alone. I envy her knowing
for certain. Forgive me.

I sit up late
after unweaving myself
and write you letters
and every time the thought comes
that you may go and I not
know about it

that I may write a month
after your death
to tell you things
as one talks meaningfully with gestures
to a friend who half a block back
has stopped at some store,
that I will hold your picture
focus on your mouth
to remember you more
while in some obscene place
a snake is crawling through your face.

I tell you my unfaithfulness
my unforgivable sin
that I am no longer sure my letters
keep you alive

but I will keep on writing
until we win
what we are fighting for
whoever we are.

IT IS NOT THAT IT CAME TO NOTHING EMILIANO

It is not that it came to nothing
Emiliano.
All things do.
It is that it came
in a slow land
so quickly true.

There is a rope
a campesino will take a tourist to see
for two pesos
that has not even rotted from the tree.

It is not that he died for nothing
Emiliano.
So all men die.
It is that he went
in a slow land
so suddenly by.

There is a temple
a precarious cone of rocks some men built here
before Christ
to please the seasons and divide the year.

It is not that your dreams died.
Dreams do.
All dreams are grass.
It is how soon
Emiliano
it came to pass.

LOG

It is Sunday.

There are two wars.

In four days
not counting border outbreaks
and rebellious acts

seventy thousand lay down dead
who were not ill or old
and did not fall off ladders.

Two blocks from where I am
words on a laundromat
appear to say

WHITE ONLY

The words are in code: they say

A DECREE WENT OUT

they say

I OWN A LAUNDROMAT AND I AM MAD

they say

KILL

It is the sign of his madness
he can write in codes
he does not know.

73

PLAIN

Out of Mobile I saw a 60 Ford
fingers wrapped like pieces of rope
around the steering wheel
foxtail flapping the head of the hood
of the first thing ever
he has called his own.

Between two Bardahls
above the STP
the flag flies backwards
Go To Church This Sunday
Support Your Local Police
Post 83
They say the same thing
They say
I am not alone.

JULY 20, 1969

I

The Los Angeles Times
The Russellville, Arkansas Courier-Democrat
The movie marquee in Pottsville, Minnesota
for instance
say Go

It is not the word
because there is no word
for what we think
are almost sure
we feel

We sit in our living rooms and see the moon tracked
by the boots of men

We knew the myth
for being something other than fact
was true

When fact and truth fall together
we say something is real
as for instance
an orange

Sermons in the city say yes
in the country no

Two o'clock in the morning
clear channel
preachers
sending grace and glory to watchmen
huddled over heaters
cooks in truckstops
old women
living alone

cry Babel
    Babel

nor stone be left on stone

Looking good. Looking good.

The Kingdom is at hand

gimme
narseena
moompie
please

II

We stand in the crowds
in the street
something like prayer
and watch the heaviest moon
come out of the clouds

I want to take off my clothes
she says
and think about them

76

they will need me here
on the face of the earth

She slides to a tree
and climbs it
like a lizard
climbing out of her clothes

She is up there somewhere

If she is still human
If it is still today in the top of the tree
she will come down

What preacher
in what poor pulpit
will look up his lines
in Fifty-Two Soul-Saving Sermons
this good coming Sunday

So What some say So What

Even a man who is pure in heart
and says his prayers at night
may become a werewolf
when the wolfbane blooms
and the autumn moon is bright

III

According to Korea's Calendar of the Moon
this is four thousand six hundred sixty-seven

Perigee to Perigee
is known as the anomalistic month

According to Korea's Calendar of the Moon
this is the Year of the Chicken
in which it is written
Admiral Peary reached the North Pole
Hitler came to power
Hitler Roosevelt Mussolini Quisling
Hiroshima and Nagasaki died
Faubus was famous
Sputnik I
little moon of mystery and a people's pride
moon of no gods
beeped its jealous way around the world
Three men flew to the moon and made a landing
A girl was born in Caruthersville, Missouri

Which may or may not be true

I report as it was reported to me
which is all an annalist can do
not understanding

IV

Earth
the coast of Africa
becoming horizon
falling away
blue planet
smooth as a catseye

Under the marbling clouds
cows are munching toward barns and the new night
are moving out to pasture
in the first light of day

Husbands and wives
argue themselves to bed
wait for the toast
stare at the table
to think what it was they said
of something to say

Soldiers in a line
lean forward
like firemen pulling a hose
move through writhing water
over deserts

The earth lifts up to meet the feet
where the line goes

Altitude 700. Drifting right.

I mean if God would of meant us to be there

Contact light. OK. Engine stop.

In Caruthersville, Missouri
a girl turned twelve
bleeds on the bed in her sleep

This day
This night This
moon's orbit
Sunday
a priest gets married
a bus goes off the road

In Santiago, Chile
Nicanor Parra
watches the low moon
sink lower
feels her behind him
turns and understands
and closes the door

By this full light
two thousand one hundred years
before we saw it
Hannibal betrayed
killed himself in Bithynia

The earth is clean from here
as in the beginning

no paperclips no bottles
no battlefields

Dave
what are you doing

no borders

nothing

one planet
perfect edges
blurred by the sun
spinning motionless through space
the first blue syllable of the unspoken word

Engine stop.
We copy you down Eagle.

Eagle

That word was coming to be
when all words were young
before the last ice left to leave to man
the Pyrenees and the Mediterranean Sea

What sound was made to say moon
in that old tongue

V

Māno / menë
Goddess of the Moon

Māno / Mōn / Mēn
Moon God of Asia

Sin
Sumerian
Moon God
Lord of All Wisdom
Lover of the Goddess Níngal
Creator of Gods

dream themselves again back into being
dream us to dream them

Sin Shamash and Ishtar
stir
come conscious

under the Palatine Hills

remember how
where   what it was
to be

feel the inpouring power
of earthly wills
saying

Sin Shamash Ishtar

saying One
saying Three

We copy you down.
Tranquility Base here.
The Eagle has landed.

The God who is God sits down
feels a sleep come on him
His woman sits down beside him
and speaks of their son

and Sin remembers Níngal
in the temple at Ur

IN COMMEMORATION OF
THE 20TH ANNIVERSARY OF
THE ED SULLIVAN SHOW
AND EVERY ANNIVERSARY FOLLOWING

Let's hear it for the Lord's Prayer

dogs dressed for dinner
dance inhumanly
but singers sing
acrobats tumble and Frank Merriwell
stands in the audience and waves.

There is gladness and ease across the land.

Absolutely, Mr. Gallagher? Positively, Mr. Sheen.

I sing you praise nobody will believe
catatonic talker for a score
of W-2s and Easters
best listener in the world
may you listen for more.
I send you praise nobody will believe
Who never wrote for Dylan Thomas
or Roethke
who never wrote a public line to grieve
for the President of the United States and Style
for Medgar Evers whose killer most nearly was mine
for Martin Luther King despised
of madmen
for Flannery O'Connor

who let my children
chase her flowering peacocks
a little while
for Robert Kennedy who was never surprised.
For all of them nothing
nothing about the war
who would have gladly
who began and began

The form can never be smaller than what it holds.
That is a fact, Flannery. Forgive the fact.

RARE FISH FOUND IN INDIAN OCEAN

Port Elizabeth, South
Africa (AP)—Rhodes
University Scientist
L.L.B. Smith, using
a color photograph,
identified a white-
blotched, velvety black
fish found in the Indian
Ocean as one of the rarest
in the world.
          Back in an aquarium
the fish died and was
eaten by crabs.

Beginning and beginning
who could write a poem about that?
The form has got to be harder than what it holds.
That is a fact, Flannery. Forgive the fact.

So saying I sing Ed Sullivan whose 20 rounds
have held the wars and The War and the children spilled
The walls of Newark darker dawn by dawn
The president killed, Evers fixed and forgotten.
Flannery gone.

Here in New Orleans only uneasily warm
sitting out only a summer thunder shower
I write for the fish I scratch in the hard dirt
the sullen stand-in
always the means to an end
and praise him to cry for all the dead children
I have cared for in fact and the act only

in bumper stickers and sit-ins and checks
and on my daughter's bedroom door, a flower.

Next week on our stage
direct from the land
where the Mustang and buffalo roam
Malcolm X
the poets Dylan Thomas and Medgar Evers
O'Connor the Catholic
the Kennedys and King
Roosevelt Jackson and all the dead children
one Homer Tuttle who sits quietly at home
and is startled to hear his name and does not understand.

HOW A SPARROW WAS CAUGHT IN MY TRAP
WHEN I WAS TEN
AND COVERED WITH LICE
SO I KILLED IT

And I recall how far I fell toward fact
to something like truth when those inlooking eyes
went to peace in the godhood of my hand

and left in me this dark and slow surprise
that gnaws like a faithful cancer at the host.
On the silent television stuck in my skull

the blind faces of children are bright as candles
the rump of a rooster gets himself up to crow
I see the soldiers crawling world without end.

The darkness in our hearts is not what we think.
We ask how this could happen. We pretend.
The darkness in our hearts is that we know.

VOICE OF AMERICA

Do not imagine his father lying
between his mother and falling to sleep
beside her while she wonders how
she knows, knowing she will keep

the secret for a weaker proof.
Do not imagine the million seed
moving by some myotic hunger
from dark to dark, from need to need.

Do not imagine one by luck
or fate finds the target to win
and like a bullet hitting a head
in slow motion crashes in.

Do not imagine the man starts
and terminates in the same act,
will be before the bullet stops
the zero absolute unfact

his mother remembered in reverse.
Do not imagine his father sent
the million missiles against the egg
with more joy and less intent.

Do not imagine the cells splitting.
Do not imagine the hollow ball
he was awhile, a senseless worm,
no heart, head, nothing at all,

as when his father a following day
the following month would ask "What is it?"
"It's nothing. It's honestly nothing at all."
Do not imagine the exquisite

danger when the cell divides
when a chromosome splits apart
half shifting here, half there,
to shape the kidney and the heart.

Do not imagine the enormous eyes.
Do not imagine the chin sits
soft against the uncovered heart.
Do not imagine the gill slits,

the hands unfinished, the tail shrinking.
Do not imagine the time at hand
or what it means. Raise the gun.
Hold it gently as you were trained

to hold it. Let the bullet swim
slowly into his opening head
fast as sperm   the way the films
in school can show a flower spread.

VS THE PEOPLE

Do you swear?

To What?

To tell the truth.

I will make distinctions
where they matter.

What is your name?

An old condition
I have not overcome.

Where were you on the night of the twenty-third?

I was committing crimes against the State.

How do you plead?

How should I know?

Think about your dog when you were seven.

And what else?

Think of the first girl you got your hands on.

And what else?

Think of the Hindenburg bursting into bloom.

And what else?

Think about two o'clock in the morning.

If that is so
yes, I confess:
I have spoken to strangers

It is my duty to warn you.

I have spread the word.
I told the preacher
the truth
I told the judge
I told the teacher telling of Abraham Lincoln
his children would know he was lying
and would eat his ears.

Who took the bomb into the power plant?

I did not vote for the president or my
mother.

Who blew up the bridge?

Jelly can be made also from apples.
The president
is in many ways my mother.

I am your mother.
What is your name?

It is still the same:
8-99-4-914.

I don't want to play
this game
anymore.

HOW THE ELEPHANT GOT HIS HUMP
FOR JOHN CHRISTMAN

Consider a fact: an olive
(unlike cherries and boysen
berries and beans) begins
as a most potent poison.

An olive grower of course
and biochemist know what'll
make it the bitter and dun
hors d'oeuvre we buy in a bottle.

The olive is soaked in lye
for twenty days and turned
on every one of the twenty
to keep it from being burned

then soaked in the juice of pickles
and turned every day
which renders the amine soluble
enough to be leached away

the amine being the problem
which amine being bound
to a protein makes an olive
which falls upon the ground

so deadly quick a poison
which is why the lye
has first to break the bond
which of course is why

no man of the Middle East
or beast has ever been seen
or seen again if he was
eating an olive green.

The question before the house:
Since the receipt is now
4,000 years old at least
who found it out, and how?

Well, I have a fancy.
Imagine the High Priest
Lord Executioner
of all the Middle East

preparing to put to death
a breaker of taboos
who diddled the temple virgins
and never paid his dues

in the shabby lodge he lived in
and pissed in the sacred pool
slept at sacrifices
and toyed with his tool

until he roused the anger
of elders and what was worse
perverse admiration
until a public curse

was said upon his head.
The High Priest swore to make
a more than common end
and set about to take

the fruit which was by custom
exquisite execution,
to cook it first in a caustic,
second an acid, solution.

When he contemplated
the agony in his hand
he could only smile
that he could understand

how he had come to be
the number one High Priest
Lord Executioner
of all the Middle East.

To make more perfect perfection
and imperfect people the humbler
he poured the *coup de grace*
two poisons in a tumbler

juice of the fruit and grain
said to drive men mad
and mixed them 5 to 1
by chance and knew he had

when he dropped in the olive
such agony in the cup
that he could scarcely speak
to summon the buglers up

to the top of the highest hill
where desert turns to sky
to summon the people in
to watch the heretic die.

The heretic being of gentle
birth albeit a fool
was set to lose his life
but would not lose his cool.

He took the drink as told to
and killed it in a swallow
and asked his host politely
if there was more to follow.

He nibbled the olive even
to take fate's roughest ration
and spat the pit at the people
and posed in a manly fashion

and was not less surprised
to find he would not die
than those prostrate about him
who called him Highest of High.

As King he showed his people
his powers were still alive
by drinking a draft of poison
each afternoon at five

for all the years of his reign
which were forty and four
and said that it was good
and often called for more

prepared of course by him
who once was Lord High Priest
who now was Royal Mixer
to the King of the Middle East.

THE HOUSE IN THE VACANT LOT

Cutting across a vacant lot
I felt concrete under my feet
and found myself at the front door
of a house that was not there anymore.

I traced the walls by where the grass
was thin and came again to the spot
where the entrance hall had been.
I let myself as it seemed to me in

and wandered through the disappeared
and long-forgotten rooms. Some glass
and a broken brick were all that was left
of the rooms where people had kissed and slept

once alone and together once.
I thought of this and then a weird
or common thought took hold of my head:
Why do I think of the past as dead?

Am I a person present and real
walking through a house that by chance
was and is not or am I he
who am not but who will be

who steps through real and present brick?
Or am I here and the house here still?
Is some woman's heartbeat quicker
when she sees the candle flicker

in a closed room? Are we together?
Does such commingling twist and crack
windows I walk through? Does a cold fear
come? Do they wonder if I walk here?

When a glass tumbles does the mother
cross herself? Does the priest
come to say that I am Christ
or to exorcise the poltergeist?

IF EVERY PERSON THERE IS BUT ONE

If every person there is but one
should disappear
and then all cats
birds grass
seahorses trees
all rocks and water and toys
and all planets the same
and the suns go out and the ashes
blow away in the winds
and the winds go
and the man explodes in bright silence
to atoms
and all the atoms dissolve to darkness
but one
which being the center
of weight and all dimension
can never
no matter how fast
move away
from the middle

that moving is not moving
We have been tricked

The atom you may say
is also nothing
and so put aside the problem
but let us say
with a fump and flash of light

and a splash of water
everything is back
and I walk across the street

by what argument do I not
when I get there
stand in dead center
still

Think of whatever moves
as God / or if nothing moves

think how still we stand

THE ASSOC. PROFESSOR (MAD SCIENTIST)
TO (HIS LOVE) HIS STUDENT
IN PHYSICS 100 LAB

What you have to know
F=MA
is what you have to know

a slow truck can break you
quick
as a fast brick

two that want love a little will lay
more likely than one
wanting love a lot

if God is anything more than simply not
he has only barely to be
so capital is the G

and you
if you turn your head
can
as a matter of course
dismiss my class

if you turned your body and
smiled
immorally illegally

I wonder
what could I do
with such a sudden force
with such a mass

I HAVE NEVER

been to a bullfight.
Sunday I saw one when the Cards were called
and nothing worth watching was happening
anywhere.

> Trumpets
> The beast
> The truth broke out like sap
> in the colored cup
> in the first of all the fights
> he was born for
>
> The monster fell in flowers
> A hard shiver
> shook out the last of his lights

Well yes, Mother.

It was black & white.

There weren't any flowers at all.

It was on the radio.

I lie a lot.

Which is what it's all about
which is not to say
I tell you anything but what is true

about the bullfight
which was in Monterrey:
the horns were a lobster's claws
the balls were blue
the sword was love in the matador's right hand.

Do you understand?

Do you understand?

IN YOUR OWN WORDS WITHOUT LYING
TELL SOMETHING OF YOUR BACKGROUND
WITH PARTICULAR ATTENTION
TO ANYTHING RELATING TO THE POSITION
FOR WHICH YOU ARE APPLYING:
PRESS DOWN

Pressing down I remember
the night my father
and mother will have forgotten:
she filled the lamps in the kitchen
he slung the washing water on the ground
chickens scattered squawking;
the sound of the pump primed
the cold zinc of the dipper
water down the chin
a mumbled word
and the long yawn at last
that leaves the body hollow as a gourd
when the vegetable skin
goes brown and hard
under the thick green vines
in the dry yard
And they went to bed
the night I came together
and began.

I may have been describing the night
my grandfather
emptied himself of my father
and my never uncles.

There was no way to tell the difference
in those nights.

I think that was the first important thing.

I was covered when I was five
like Job with boils
they shaved my head
peeled the cloth away from the bed
in the morning.
I slept
propped on hands and knees
my mother kept me clean
my forehead against the floor
the doctor stayed
while my father who was a
preacher prayed.
The neighbors came to call
said What have you done
that God has put this affliction on your son.

When I was eleven I went to sleep
with a gothic radio underneath the quilt
the glowing grin of the dial
bright as the guilt I manufactured there.

Saturday night the Grand Old Hayride
There's A Great Speckled Bird
Flying Somewhere
But I Didn't Hear Nobody Pray.

Sunday nights I listened to the prophets,
how faith washes sins and Catholics away:

This is Brother Bob's Good Old Gospel Hour
Our time is almost
send your dimes and dollars
The Bible Man
B-I-B-L-E
We depend
to help us carry on
to the first two thousand
a plastic table cloth
that glows
in the dark
with the face of Jesus

Imagine what your friends and neighbors will say

while the choir sings one more time
in the background softly

and tenderly Jesus is calling
O Sinner Come Home.

Monday Miss Gardner began the fifth grade
took up the marbles
let Big Butt Butler erase the board
never me
sent sealed messages to other rooms
by Salina Mae who was already starting
to have tits Walter said were got
from doing it.

O. D. showed what he had behind the gin
always after Salina Mae was gone
and Mary Sue let us look if we begged her.

107

Walter drowned.
O. D. is a doctor. Mary Sue married
a preacher and has children.
Salina Mae I will tell you about.

One Saturday Afternoon we made believe

That is all I can tell

On my grandfather's farm
there was a river we swam in
there was an old bell to call us back

MY FATHER WHO IS SEVENTY-FIVE
WILL NOT THANK GOD FOR HIS YEARS

> ". . . children ardent for some
> desperate glory. . . ."
>
> WILFRED OWEN

He imagines how a child not his
crawls across the floor
and calls his name
bubbles into flame and disappears

He imagines the smell in his kitchen
of smoldering hair
imagines that burning fingers
curl like snakes

He sleeps to see me standing in the door
blazing

He wakes to find me not there
and alive
is embarrassed to be glad

I know that he is

But come to seventy-five my father
will not thank God for anything that is his

DURING A LANGUAGE LESSON: FOR KAREN

What is it that a genius knows?
Karen there are mostly those
who talk parabolas I suppose
but others if only a very few
say wissenschaft

not as men of science do.
What genius are you pointing to?
The one that in a season drew
the bright curving of your clothes
by wiccecraeft?

AT THE END OF MY THIRTY-NINTH YEAR

I

I came
being no country's king
without a bugle or flag or drum
or angels to sing
or anything
not even silver in my eyes
the eighth day of the fourth month
when the only thing to fear was fear
though my father would not know that
for another year.

There was no sign
for my aunts to see
in the cow's milk or the dog's hair
that I should be blest
and loved or curst
so they laid me down and left me there
equally out of hope and despair
to nothing but luck and the New Deal
and the mercy of God and my mother's breast.

The cards were all cornered.
Fear was a radio that eats the earth.

But luck and mercy have lasted.

My brothers came home.

111

She was not pregnant.

I am almost forty.

II

All of which is a way of saying look.

III

A friend has come by after twenty years.
I am a little sadder than before he came.
The nervous socialist no longer moves
across my memory when I think the name.

He has come into my house and killed himself.
He is here. He is not. It has been too long.
He sits with his wife as we trade remembering
and looks at me as if I remember wrong.

IV

When mercy grows tired of mercy or luck fails
let me remember in all hospitals jails
let me remember rightly your hands and feet
the places where your nakedness and mine meet

that we are together here a better time
than luck even alone or mercy can bear
which is to say I have not understood
the meaning of this or the meaning of anything much

of the sign in the cow's milk that was not there
to tell of anything or the dog's hair
except as there are no signs. Except as we breathe.
Except as we barely touch. And leave off breathing.

A LETTER TO CINDY, ROBERT & KAREN

Being various precepts and admonitions
toward a good life and perhaps long

Against lessons learnt
against plans for war
actuarial tables
the good sense of remembering nothing

I set this down:

there is a capsule I will bury
to be found
when it is old enough to be important.
This as you know now was in it.

I have only eleven things to tell you.

Cindy first, a reminder. Write it down.
In the beginning was the word
and the word was withdrawn.
Which brings me to your question

about the aluminum temple in New York:
the answer is no.

Robert:
Learn to kick.

If you aren't that mad you will lose anyway.
Go home.

Most girls had rather be kissed
inside the elbow
but the tip of the tongue on the corner of her mouth
will do it.
You have known this for a long time.

Karen: Be careful of trucks coming toward you
of mad men with knives
of policemen. They are necessary
to full employment and a sane nation.
Do not trust them.

When you begin to drive
as you have done
what you must remember is this
about the young man
who at the corner of Canal and Magazine
lets you in line:
he has been a part of your life a moment.
You will never see him again.
When he has gone to bed
twenty thousand times
with the same woman
lost ten thousand hands
of poker and his teeth
you will not be a wrinkle
in his brain
who held him long enough
from some sudden intersection
once.
Think of this when you learn to drive.

And for the three of you these three things:

Remember your names and the names of your
grandfathers.
Remember the hills of earth.

There is a story you will have to read. Read it.

I have gone past eleven.

We love you. I tell you this directly and
without embarrassment.
Try not to think about it too much.

LOVE POEM

Six o'clock and
the sun rises across the river.
The traffic cop wakes up and
crawls over his wife.
The naked professor will sleep another hour.
The dentist wakes up and reaches for a smoke.
The doctor reaches for the phone
and prescribes
his voice full of rust.
The shoeclerk wakes to his clock
touches himself
and lies listening to his woman in the shower.

It is midnight now in Samoa.

Nine o'clock and
the school bell rings.
Miss Gardner taps her ruler on the desk.
She calls the roll.
Oscar Carpenter is absent.
He does not like the sound of the ruler.

It is midnight now in Osaka.

Eleven o'clock:
The salesman makes his way past dogs and wheels
his knuckles already sore
hoping for bells

On Maple Street the policeman's wife
shuts her kimono slowly and shuts the door.
On Willow Street the professor's wife
tells him about her cousin in Mineral Wells
who was also a salesman but never amounted to much.

On Juniper Street the dentist's wife
is drunk and lets him have her on the floor
says she will get a divorce
says she will see him again of course if she can.

It is midnight now in Djakarta.

Five o'clock and
the men are coming home.
The traffic cop comes home
his ears in his pockets.
The doctor comes home
the sun slipping down his forehead.
The shoeclerk comes
The uncertain knees
still fitting the socket of his eyes.

It is midnight now in Berlin.

Six o'clock:
The streetlights come on.

It is midnight now in Bordeaux.

Ten o'clock:
In Mercy Hospital a man is dying.
His brain
squeezes all his thoughts to one thought

squeezes that to nothing
and lets go.

It is midnight now in La Paz.

Eleven o'clock:
The children are gone to bed and we are here
sitting across the room from one another
accustomed to this house
that is not ours to keep
to this world that is not ours
and to each other.

Sands run through the children in their sleep.

New Poems

LEAVING NEW YORK
ON THE PENN CENTRAL TO METUCHEN
FOR JIM WHITEHEAD

Go buck, go hiss and the bright bolted works
tremble and turn. Go clank and the car jerks,

grabs at the tracks and moves off underground.
Sealed in a tube of light, we ride the sound

for something to ride. We stare into the black
unsteady glass and see ourselves stare back.

And then we rise. Timetables will tell
that we have risen. But there's no hell if hell

does not receive the leakage of this place.
Nor punishment for sin nor sin nor grace.

A milky head still bounces in the dense
expensive air: closed roads, a gateless fence,

walls of windows, every one gone blind
pass through it like visions through a distracted mind.

Here we are she said it's just a room
Gases, like ghosts turned out of a broken tomb,

form faces, halves of faces, ears and eyes
while brimstone burns and jagged slagheaps rise

like bony tumors. Each of us is going
to some green place in sunlight, secure in knowing

what schedules tell, what signs go by outside.
She is waiting somewhere while I ride

backward bumping in this trembling crowd
whose hands hold papers and whose heads are bowed

as if in prayer, though I imagine not.
More likely they are thinking of a lot

of simple things like is it going to rain
and what to tell her if she meets the train.

THINK OF JUDAS THAT HE DID LOVE JESUS
FOR WALTER WEISS

I

Think of Judas that he did love Jesus
that he for simple grace came and for glory
out of a thinness of days to a mad band
that he was filled of his fathers and full with fury
that it came to him to force the Master's hand
that it came to him to have the battle begun
that it came to him that when the Lord will have won
he would see the son of Man a King
who being gentle would not have had it done
for all the helmets split and the blood spilled.

Think that when he sees how Christ is killed
he does the only thing he knows to do
goes not with God but goes another way
from the plain man he never meant to betray.

II

Or think of Judas filled with sin and fears
afraid to tell his name, or name the burning
torments turning like scorpions over his skin.

Think that Jesus who needs to be betrayed
chooses anxious Judas for his friend
and uses Judas to God's and the devil's end.

123

Think how Judas knows that Jesus knew
knowing all hearts what Judas would come to do.
Think that Judas recognizes the role
played half in shadow with a short line to speak
knows he is poor of spirit and sufficiently weak
for which and no plain love he was called to this.

Curses Christ who knowing he was faithful
to both their purposes cast him for such a kiss.

Curses himself who curses first the Lord
who alone is the Lord and leads himself away
with a bought rope from trust he did not betray.

III

Or think of Judas. As anyone can tell
Judas is bad. Jesus is good and betrayed
for cash and badness. Judas is afraid
and finds a tree and hangs himself upon it
and holds his fist that none of the fee fall
to the watchful beggars. His name is lust for money
disgrace before God and men and broken trust.
Is shame. Is everlasting as the unspoken name.

IV

These are the stories of Judas that fill the spaces
inside the story of Judas. Look quickly
behind the words you have heard and uncover creatures
looking the other way with words in their hands.

Unseen hearts of Herod therefore and of Caesar
and even of us.   Or is it better

to listen to the preachers, what they say
believing in the gospel but not in the ghosts
haunting our histories our papers our simplest books
turning invisibly toward us at every word
with round incredulous and desperate looks.

THINKING FRIDAY NIGHT
WITH A GOTHIC STORM GOING ABOUT
FINAL CAUSES AND LOGOS AND
MITZI MAYFAIR

Was the Word and the Word was just
a swelling in the ether. Dust

that would seem wind, sun, earth and sea
had not come to seem to be

and ether was only force compacted.
So are we. Though we have acted

like Stuff, we know that we are not.
We are spume and a sunspot.

This man that seems to know its name
is a water spout, a flame,

a whirlpool, a funnel storm
where nothing stays except the form

the funnel is. We are nothing
but energy in love, come huffing

and puffing our way through what we take
as time and space, as wine and steak.

This is philosophy I think
and science and a waste of ink.

And still I know the shape I touch
that seems something is nothing much,

is only a moving, and we are dreams
we have about us. The earth that seems

rocks and water is only force
moving through a shape. The source,

they will say, of rhyme and the seasons
but we have our own good reasons

for holding to the old confusions
of form and thing. What but illusions

matter at all when all things
are what they do? A wasp's wings,

for instance, and you, as I am a node
energy moves through, coming as food

drink, salt, sunlight, air,
and leaving as heat, spit, hair,

tears, toenails, words and sperm.
Lord bless the lowly worm

who is also form in flux
and does not know or care and fucks

such as he does without the stinking
thoughts we always come to thinking.

127

Darling, let us learn to move
like that again—apparent you

force and form, *vis-à-vis*
form and force, apparent me—

riding the storm all words are about
till the storm stops. Played out.

IF I SAID I LOVE YOU WOULD YOU? NO.

If I said I love you would you? No.
Far too many men have told me so.

If I said I need you would you then?
A hollow fist can fill the needs of men.

If I said I want you? I'm no fish
pulled from the sea to grant a fisher's wish.

If I paid you, then would you consent?
You would whisper where your money went.

Then you will never share my bed? I might
to hold back the invasions of the night.

But this is morning, and the sun is slow.
I know it is, but where the sun will go

it is not yet, and I am a trembling tree
to think how dark the streets of Rome must be.

FOR BECKY WITH LOVE
THE EIGHTH YEAR OF THE SLAUGHTER
A Minuet for Army Boots and Orchestra

Whose tongues are twisted and whose hearts are shrunk
may play as puppets, may in that disguise
while villages burn in their brains, drink to be drunk.

So when God comes to catch this crumbling chunk
of dirt, what do we say? That we despise
whose tongues are twisted and whose hearts are shrunk?

If Thomas had told us the gnawed body stunk,
what would it change? Men knowing what men devise
while villages burn in their brains, drink to be drunk.

If Calvin came to tell us Christ is bunk,
what could he hope to teach us? Pain? Surprise?
Whose tongues are twisted and whose hearts are shrunk?

So the viking sails for home and is sunk,
so Napoleon is poisoned, so Lorca dies,
while villages burn in their brains. Drink to be drunk

until they lay us to sleep and slam the trunk,
two people more who open and close their eyes,
whose tongues are twisted and whose hearts are shrunk,
while villages burn in their brains. Drink to be drunk.

HURRAH FOR THE FUN
IS THE PUDDING DONE
HURRAH FOR THE PUMPKIN PIE

The Hummingbird Hill
Geriatric Center

where cars come crunching
over gravel
Sundays

filled with faces of children
about to be bored

by the superannuated
by the old people

whose ragged heads
shake
no no no
at nothing

whose hands
in their hollow laps
jerk and settle like
abandoned boats

who spit in paper sacks
who drop their teeth
who forget the names of children

131

was called
before the war

The Hancock County Home
for Old People

Which is the true name

No such blurred wings
have been seen
hovering here

not even by Catherine Bilderback
who sees all things

who sees her husband come early
home from Houston

who sees girls climbing trees
in the broom closet

who sees frogs
dropping from the ceiling
buzzing about her like great
green flies

who sits for hours by her window
waiting

until her husband
disguised
as a dark attendant

wakes her saying
did you go to the bathroom

VISION AND PRAYER

Christ that as the maggot
Takes unto himself our putrefaction
Cleanse us now and in the hour of our death

Christ that as the maggot
Comes not for the clean
Cleanse us now and in the hour of our death

Christ that as the maggot
Comes from the grave and grows wings
Cleanse us now and in the hour of our death

Christ that as the maggot
Is with us always
Cleanse us now and in the hour of our death

Maggot of God that eats away
The corruption of the world
Cleanse Bless us now and in the hour of our death

REMEMBERING WALTER

I remember when I learned he was dead.
I was halfway done with a paper route
and saw the crowd and stopped to find out
what was going on and someone said

Walter was drowned. I had to go disguised
in a borrowed boy scout uniform to take
my turn sitting beside him at the wake,
to halfway hope the skin across his eyes

would tighten against the light. I would find mud
to bless them open or find whoever knew
what it was you had to say or do.
But someone said he didn't have his blood.

What should these memories mean at forty-two?
The twelve is a highly impressionable age.
That all the rage we learn is the first rage.
That more than choose to die by water, do.

FOR KENNETH PATCHEN

I understand the pain as well as most.
No one could want you to stay for more of that.
Or more of us either, for that matter,
heroes busy with history busy with flat

lying towns and soldiers with quick hands.
I think I know what it is to say whatever
it was you said and wait for three wars
to see something happen that happens never.

I understand I think what it is to leave
the one that wishes only you could wait.
I believe I know what it is to let go
the whole phenomenological world, to say

this is the end. After this is nothing.
No fingertips. No curious brow. No breast.
I understand I think what it is to die.
What I have not understood is death.

Which is why it makes me sad, your dying.
The verb I understand. It's a going down.
But death is a darker thing. And you Kenneth Patchen
almost made us understand the noun.

PROBLEMS IN THE SPACE-TIME CONTINUUM: UNDISCOVERED LETTERS TO MITZI MAYFAIR

If in the future
a time traveller
comes back to this moment
he's here now

If I could be
in two places at once
I would be with you twice
all the time

At 35,000 feet
you see a car
run off a lost road and turn over
what do you tell the stewardess
her arms full of coffee

No one will remember you always
the insects are going to take over

There will come a year
when one by one your friends
thumbing past your last address
will think to mark through it

This nausea that opens in my throat
like a morning glory
shows that I am still alive and
can want you

136

AND THEN

Your toothbrush won't remember your mouth
Your shoes won't remember your feet

Your wife one good morning
will remember your weight
will feel unfaithful
throwing the toothbrush away
dropping the shoes in the Salvation Army box
will set your picture in the living room

Someone wearing a coat you would not have worn
will ask was that your husband
she will say yes

THE NEIGHBOR

No one knows what the banging is all about
or the drilling that buzzes like a swarm of gnats
above the clover between his woods and the wash

or why it is he never came into the store
to pick up his almanac
or goes to Grange anymore

or why his sons have all come back from the city
and their fair wives with them

or why he walks the long fences of his farm
picking up sometimes a twig
turning it in his fingers
and letting it fall.

The main fact is which does make us uneasy
he's set about building something in his barn

and it's big.

CABBALA

> We shall not all sleep
> but we shall all be changed
> I Cor. 15:51

He will try to make you believe he's alive.
He will watch the way you move
remembering how it was with muscle and bone
but he will be uncertain, he will hesitate
like a man who has been in bed for a long time.

You may recognize him in this way.

At first if you listen he will ask
innocent questions.
If you answer them he will agree with you
whatever you say.

He will look for a way to touch you
his skin to your skin
something perfectly natural and unnoticed.

A man folding a paper at a bus stop
asking what you think of the cost of living
bumps your hand.

If he pulls you into conversation
you may hear a voice beneath the voice
having nothing to do with the present talk
or this town.

139

If you hear such a voice
you will know the man is in reality dead.

When he knows that you know
he will do one of two things.

He will open his face.
He will call the name nobody knows you by
over and over
backing away from the bus stop
backing safely into the flow of the traffic
letting out the syllables like a fisherman's line.

This is not too bad if you can take it
but it may not be in your case
what he does.
The simple alternative there is no point
in telling.

If you are asleep when he sees you
almost surely you will not get on the bus.
If he comes to you in a dream
try to wake up.

If he catches you in command of yourself
at the corner of some bright ordinary street
maple leaves and fire hydrant and all the right cracks
in the sidewalk
you must try to wake up anyway.

I GO OUT OF THE HOUSE FOR THE FIRST TIME

I go out of the house for the first time
since the day everybody found out
and the first person I meet says hello turd
so I pull off my ears I have always had
distinctive ears and drop them in a trash
dispenser in front of The Farmers Bank and a man
coming out of the bank says hello turd
so I twist off my nose as people have always
noticed my nose in particular and drop it in
the book deposit in front of the city library
and a woman coming out of the library says
hello turd and I begin to see
how difficult disguises are and pluck
my left eye out as people have always noticed
my eyes are most particularly well-matched
and swallow it down as there is no place to put it
and a small boy up a lamp pole says
hello turd so I take off my clothes
as people have always commented on my clothes
and I walk down the street and a little girl
playing jacks on the sidewalk sees me and says
hello turd so I pull off my penis
and everybody runs up saying in loud voices
look at the dumb turd he pulled off his penis

A TOAST TO FLOYD COLLINS

To Mitzi Mayfair
To Jesus Christ Man of A Thousand Faces
To Len Davidovich Trotsky
To Nicanor Parra

To whoever dies tonight in New Orleans
To Operator 7 in Kansas City

To the sound of a car crossing a wooden bridge
To the Unified Field Theory
To the Key of F

And while I'm at it
A toast to Jim Beam
To all the ice cubes thereunto appertaining
To Becky knitting
A silver cat asleep in her lap
And the sun going down

Which is the explanation for everything

ON THE SYMBOLIC CONSIDERATION OF HANDS
AND THE SIGNIFICANCE OF DEATH

Watch people stop by bodies in funeral homes.
You know their eyes will fix on the hands and they do.
Because a hand that has no desire to make
a fist again or cut bread or lay stones
is among those things most difficult to believe.
It is believed for a fact by a very few
old nuns in France who carve beads out of knuckle bones.

VISION IN BLACK AND WHITE

Leaning back in a Naugahyde
covered recliner
reading proofs

I flash on my father stepping carefully
in hightop shoes
in nineteen hundred and twelve

across a road
all wagon tracks and mud
alive in the sun

to someone waiting on the other side
I think a woman

I give my attention to him
and the image breaks
I go back to my proofs
and he starts across again

The problem is not to notice
The problem is to let him go

ABOUT THE AUTHOR

MILLER WILLIAMS was born in Hoxie, Arkansas. He lives with his wife and three children in Fayetteville, Arkansas, and teaches in the creative writing program at the University of Arkansas. In addition to his poetry he has achieved note as a translator, most recently with a translation of the poems of Nicanor Parra: *Emergency Poems*, and as an anthologist, serving as editor of the new anthology, *Contemporary Poetry in America*.

DATE DUE

GAYLORD   PRINTED IN U.S.A.